POETICALLY EXPOSED...

Lianne Wambui

authorHOUSE®

AuthorHouse™
1663 Liberty Drive
Bloomington, IN 47403
www.authorhouse.com
Phone: 1-800-839-8640

First published by AuthorHouse   09/12/2011

ISBN: 978-1-4567-5147-0 (sc)
ISBN: 978-1-4567-5148-7 (ebk)

Library of Congress Control Number: 2011908013

Printed in the United States of America

1.

Pin me against the wall
and ravage my lips
separate their innocence
and discover…
Close your eyes.
Bite.
Slowly sink yourself in their sweetness
arrest my tongue.
Tango.

2.

Come let's…kiss
come, touch my soft lips
let's…consummate
engage in our secret dissections
propositions…submissions.

3.

I love the taste of your lips
I just can not help it
I love being lost in their sweet surrender.

4.

My lips are curious
they want to know yours
but you hesitate,
scared of the overwhelming feeling
the union may bring-
But I continue…
unaware of your uneasy thoughts.
Totally oblivious
I just want a taste,
- an embrace
of the deep icing that graces this cake…
-Let me kiss you.

5. Mozart revived.

Your hands will write a symphony
notes of love on this beautiful body
tones that star the night
tempos that birth light.

Your hands will spin heavenly music
melodies to water these parched lips
from the keys you play- I take a sip
and let your song from my lips drip.

6.

Under the street's light
his touch stopped her tracks,
and their quick glance turned into a stare
as a probable kiss lingered in the air.

Under the street's light
their world became still,
as he tried to inhale her frame
her name and from where she came.

Under the street's light
these strangers held hands,
as their attraction-
they tried to understand.

Under the street's light,
this handsome night's knight
had come to save this damsel
- from her plight.

7. Infatuation?

Stab my heart.
Pry this rib cage open
grab my heart
-rip it from within.

Squeeze this heart
watch the pain dive to the earth
breathe my heart
and inhale its love- now your life.

8. *The struggle*

I am biting hard, hard on to what I know,
but the more I ponder of you, my grasp wanes.
Your light hath begun to slowly seep through,
and hath begun to part my eyelids in two…

The path I daily plod, many have stepped,
tis' the path of immaturity, a path without depth,
I now struggle to break from my tarnished self,
and follow your staff to a place of wealth.

9. Bike lover.

Passionate sensations bleed through my veins
as I sit and caress your reins.
Handles so smooth, so tight
I grasp; bracing myself for the flight
rims smile as we cruise the streets
filling each observing heart with an ecstatic beat.

One. We submerge into each other
the leather on my back, now your brother
rubber to road, a threat to the weather
we kiss the horizon, together.

10. *When you kiss me.*

Plant a kiss so sweet and wet
that when you leave I'll never forget
thoughts of bliss in my mind let
drops of sweat, down my spine melt.

I'm captured in this moment.
Enjoying each minute of Love's beautiful torment
these feelings- one of a kind
engulf me and blow my mind.
Kiss.

Kissing me...
Your luscious lips refresh mine
Like frozen drops in summer time,
I said when you leave I think about you all the time
all the time… all the time.

11. *My love for you grows…*

I
Love you.
So very much-
I put myself apart
from every such and such.
I know you're God's work- art,
a masterpiece, from the heavens above.
Breath taking, soul consuming, being of love,
may I be whisked away in your tender loving arms.

12.

My lips reached for a closer view
at first a trickle on the toes
then a total plunge in the blue.

Like a deep sea diver
I reached for the depths
of these sensual waters-
and explored your caves beneath.

13. Innocent

Reflections of blue birds flying outside my window
shadows of masked creatures in the grass below,
voiced threats remind me I'm a prisoner in my home
barred behind my doors, I have no place to roam.

The fruits of my loins lie dead asleep
looking up I pray, their souls you may keep.
I pace in their blood, yelling out in a manner absurd,
but their souls continue to linger, in the heavens above.

My stained hands are alive with sweat,
as their eyes paint the story - the pain they felt.
The voices outside fill my heart with torment
as breaths of fear engulf this moment.

Who will believe my white words gestured in red hands,
that attempts to revive, were made by lifeless hands?
I have no place to run, no place to turn,
so I open the door and praise the sky,
but they shoot.

14.

I'd love to kiss you
just once.
A soft simple connection
for a minute, two, maybe three?

I'd love to hold you
for a while…
feel your heart in sync with mine
and watch you smile.

I'd love to love you
for a lifetime,
and simply be
your companion
for eternity.

15.

I love you
but you do not know,
you love me
but do not show.

At each other we glance
with similar thoughts,
yet keep holding back
love's effortless efforts.

I love you.
I will let you know.
You love me,
you will eventually show.
At each other we will glance
with similar thoughts,
and in love's consuming trap
be forever caught.

16.

It was just a touch on the lips,
but I felt a tingle in my toes
It was just an ordinary day,
but it began with a rose.

The things you did, were like fairy tales told
from the ride in the carriage, to the ring of gold.
dinner under the moon, made your feelings unfold
warm words floated, like sweet scent flows.

You sowed sensuous feelings, now my love grows
buds in my heart bloom in radiant red rows,
beautiful hopes are brewed in this pleasure-
Oh what beautiful ropes, to my newly found treasure.

17. *Unwelcome guest*

Sadness knocked on my door tonight
and I opened, for I was a far from joy's delight.
She settled in my heart's middle, right in sight
and unloaded her belongings from yesterday's flight.

My radiant walls were absorbed by her icy touch
pleasant memoirs dried, leaving nothing but a dry patch.
Hope's fresh scents -putrid from her petty such and such
the suffering she shared was just too much.

Her conquest did not end at the source,
for she sought more vulnerable land with no remorse.
She bore and tore,
left my mind in painful flaw,
tarnished drapes no longer to adore,
tarnished hopes- I dream no more.

18. *Drought's cry.*

Spit on us Mother Nature.
Bring rays of hope from our Creator.
Our land has become bare,
the blazing sun does not spare,
we have tried to escape from this lion's lair,
but the pain is too much to bear.

The fissures of the earth kiss those of our feet.
the food in our mouths is the air we breathe,
sour sweat sadly sowed- has failed to conceive
and now the bones of our being are hard to conceal.

Clouds above, cry on us…
Wail torrents of life to relieve this curse.

19. *My diamond in the dirt...*

You caught my eye from the moment I saw you
patiently you lay beneath the rocks that held you
the sparkle in your eye lit a fire in my heart
and the light rose through the deathly darkness of my earth.

You caught my eye from the moment I saw you
lying in the dirt, I was tempted to touch you
but you lay fast beneath the rocks that held you
so I kissed the ground and slept beside you.

20. Rendezvous.

My hands will caress your face,
give your lips a taste of heavenly grace.
My eyes will be lost in yours,
as a drop of water in rolling waterfalls.
My lips can't wait to say "I do,"
so that I can hold you and entirely unfold you.

21. *Life.*

You fell by the wayside,
in the only race that ever mattered.

22. Bathroom bowl reunions.

I burst through the door
looking for my mid-morn companion
the time has come,
this court is now in session.

I bend down and hug you,
In your face I kiss my reflection.
It feels good, I feel great,
as you listen to my bile stained conversation.

The room fills with the sour stench,
the sour stench- my fermented breath
you squarely face my twisted face
my twisted face in drunken state.

23. *A rumor*

The whispers stain the air
and float to the valley so flawless and fair,
the sparkling stream takes a sip
and is turned to mud- tough and thick.

Black notes tarnish the skies
beautiful doves now seem like flies,
the silver lining of their precious lives
rusts and withers and sadly dies.

Raindrops from above, crash in torrents
waves birthed seize these moments
the beautiful green that once peacefully lived,
now lies beneath the dark waters that seethe.

24. Obsession.

You are always on my mind
I want to stop everything I'm doing,
come to where you are and just hold you…

Your words are caring and kind,
they travel the distance between us
and drop a kiss of life into my soul…

We will forever be entwined,
bound in unbreakable cords
of love and hope…

You are always on my mind-
the reason I sing…
my love, my dream.

25. My love.

My love will be more than the waters of the seas
abundant and wealthier than kings and queens.
My love will shine like the morning sun
illuminating the depths of the skies and land.
My love will be strong like Samson's hand
and will carry you through the twists and turns.
My love will be there through thick and thin
a high ground to stand when storms are in.

26.

If I could draw your picture,
the paper would melt at the beauty of your smile

If I could sing to you,
the sun would beg to stay and fade all darkness away

If I could write about you,
I would fill endless pages about your undying love throughout the ages

If I could hold you now,
my hands would never let go…
-My lips would not know how.

27. *A minute late.*

I had an argument
words flew around, filling the heart with torment
anger burst and boiled- I needed a moment.

When I came back, you were gone
I called out for you- my son
but you did not return.

Silence whispered impending doom
as I opened the door to your room
and there you looked at me, teary eyed
as the smooth silk curtain kissed your neck's side.

28. *Tearless*

I won't sink my face into the pillow
I won't run away into the willow
I won't hide under my darkest fears
I won't cry for you…

I won't sit here waiting by the window
I won't close myself behind my room's door
I won't cry myself to sleep again…
I won't die for you…

29.

When I look at you
sadness wells in my heart
I don't love you
and that's a fact.

When you look at me
it tears you apart
you can't have me
the reality is that.

30.

I send you a rose…
a rose for every minute I think of you
a rose for every moment away from you
a rose to show how much I'm in love with you…

My love can not be described by mere, mere words,
it has drilled through my bones and struck at my heart.
I'm going insane, my life's falling apart
I love you, have loved you- right from the start.
So I send you a rose,
so red, it glows.
A rose plucked from my soul
where love blooms and grows.
A rose for you
watered with words of truth
a rose everlasting- I love you.

31. Color blind.

When you look at me
what do you see?
do you see the curves in my eyes?
does my hue take you by surprise?
or do you see my heart-
A heart that beats like yours
a heart that sings in joy
that bleeds when hurt…
as you look at me
I hope you see
a people one at heart
a people one in mind
as you look at me,
I hope you see
you in me.

32. Page one…

I open a new page in my life
a new chapter birthed in light
plain plains, oh so white
on which my pencil softly glides
    A new page, an era unfolds
    a new love, someone to hold
    a breath of life, a kiss of joy
    a new chapter with pleasures untold.

33. Love undying.

If you'll be mine
you'll make me the happiest man in the world
If you turn me away,
you'll leave me dying…
I'll be torn from the greatest love I've ever had.

34.

I know it's not Valentine's Day,
but please be mine.
It's snowing and frozen outside
but can I come and spend some time.
I will walk through a storm to be where you are
sacrifice my all, to roll my fingers through your hair.
All I need to hear is that you care
that whenever I reach out, you'll be there
my heart has never loved like this before
It waits to have and hold you,
and love you even more.

35.

I softly kiss your lips
again and again
and my thirst is quenched
again and again.

The moments our lips share
leave us speechless, breathless
the silenced sighs made
leave me weak, helpless.

I am falling fast; I cannot help it,
Love's hand reaches out,
I take it.

You got me thinking of you
more than I think of myself
I am in love with you
and nobody else.
You had my heart
right from the start
nothing on this earth
can tear us apart.
You're on my mind, all the time
a light in the dark- my sunshine
I can't live without you- my lifeline
I love you, I love you
Please be mine.

37. Let my lonely heart sleep.

I hope you're not making me fly
only to take my wings away.

I hope you're not taking me high
to blow clouds my way.

Don't steal the smile
that hides tears from last night,

don't awaken my heart
to kiss it goodnight.

38. Why

I trust no one.
trust lived here years ago
but packed her things
and left my eyes, my soul.

She loved second chances
loved accepting at first glances
but she was deceived so many a times,
her trusting eyes became blind,
welcoming lips made mime.

Constant lies tore at her beauty
ate away with no remorse or pity.
She was left weak, broken, dying
and now lays forsaken, like a rusted dime.

Trust lives here no more
she left, and my heart is now frozen, cold.

39. In turn.

Let your shirt fall off your shoulders
and I will let my ribbon free my hair
whisk me away with that smile so bright
and I will make your heart dance in the morning light

Laugh like you knew not of sorrow
and I will sing like there is no tomorrow
kiss with a passion to make my soul fly
and I will love in a fashion to kiss your tears dry.

40. A balance imbalanced

You can go to the moon
While my five children starve

Build buildings and trains
But no valve for my heart

I sent my sons to war
While yours played in the yard

Our perfect balance and yet so imbalanced.

My home is still flooded
You just bought new land

On my roof baby scurried
While you waived from above

The skies were bright
But our dark faces missed your Reserve

What a perfect imbalance to this imbalance.

Nine to five coins barely touch healing hands
Yet fifty two mill' can pay a gamer's hand

You collect, we pay
For benefits in foreign lands

Why you take so much from none
I still cannot understand.

Millions die daily of Aids
But one magic star survives

My two year old is on chemo
'a fifty year old biker got new life'

They rejected my A's in Law school
But took your C to preside...

Oh how can't we see this imperfection in our perfect balance?

Abortion made my mother
Eject me half alive

I waited patiently in the darkness
only to be welcomed by a doctor's scythe

You heard my feeble cries
but lay there- a cold distant look in your eyes

This twisted balance we call life
has made you a mother to a lifeless life.

41.

Approach, slowly, and softly kiss…
let our lip union commence behind closed doors-
a speech of silent words.

My clothes slowly surrender
to the whispers from our tongues
The voice in my ear- oh so tender
makes my bound feelings erupt in splendor.

42. No man's land

Again I arrived
at no man's land
Its touch of limbo
embraces my hand.

The odor of this place
I can not understand
a void land- a space
where love has no ground.

No man's land
he loves me, I don't
no man's land,
I love him, he does not.

43.

I do not love you
no not now,
but I will try to love
as you dig this heart with plough.

I hear not the bells of eternity
no not now
but I will incline mine ear
as you whisper into my heart's fear.

I do not see the white picket fence
the three room house on the hill,
or the dog…
but I see you, and I will try first, to love.

44.

I will overlook the grand ship
my choice of craft,
and simply sail love's waters
with this raft.

The waters will kiss my feet
as I flee from the rapids of my past,
but I will slowly journey on
hoping that this time
this love will last.

45.

And he knew what he wanted
as he sat next to her
stolen smiles exchanged
he made her wonder
those lips...those eyes...those lips.

And their silent conversation
only lasted but a few
but the special moment they had shared
had been watered- and silently grew
that second...that moment...that time.

And the distance between them
had a story to tell
but they each kept a memory
of the moment they fell
those words...those eyes...those lips.

And as they plunged-
soaking into each others arms
he knew...she could tell
it could be
that moment...that time...worthwhile.

46. Foster home Fridays…

Another warm day
drops snow flakes in my heart,
and with the window as my canvas
and my finger- the paint brush
I draw a smiley face
- I love you mum-

Another dry day
floods my pillows with tear drops,
I feel so alone
and my mum's smiling face in the window
Is now gone…

Another blue-skied day
throws hail storms my way
cold cutting winds
lash at my rosy cheeks
as I press on the warm window
waiting for her to come home.

Another day, an ordinary day
brings a car up the drive way
and I secretly hope
they will take this pain away.

47. Plaisirs doux.

Prisoner of passion
bound to the beams of love.
Slave to seduction,
'twined and tethered to its seams.

Maid of the moment,
pleasured by pain.
Wrapped in layers of lust,
patiently you await the touch and thrust.

Bound to the bed of a beggar
strapped down in leather,
you toss and you turn
for his bold body you yearn.

The chains rip at your flesh.
You try to catch your breath.
Dripping with sweat, engulfed in sweet pain,
the pleasure so intense, it explodes your brain.

48. shelter under a Bush.

Uplifted by the most high, made a ruler
selected by many, you promised to lead us,
but when trials attacked, you were gone,
a people were deserted, left in the storm.

Homes were destroyed,
they were left unemployed,
they ate in filth; while you sat back and enjoyed,
poor mothers were dying, children were crying,
weren't the people of New City, citizens' abiding?

Plans were being made, star studded boys doing their work,
but it took longer to arrive, than it took to Iraq.
As I watched the news, only one color I saw
the color of beauty, the color of flaw.

Now we realize, that we were all wrong,
to hide under a Bush, instead of a tree strong.

49.

Yes!
We all have sad days
but we have to accept the cards dealt.
One night brings drenched pillows
but the next morning, you must rise.

You have to be strong and wake up,
let the sun kiss your tear stained face
let the wind mess your hair
Insist to revive the flickering desire in you
to dance…
to sing…
to love…

50.

I climb the hill,
sometimes I slide and spill
my cup of coffee against my will
sometimes I trip on a rock
and my face kisses the hard, cold earth
I will not let this deter me from my path.

I climb the hill
it is tough.
dreams are crushed when I get to the top and find
more paths, more earth
more goals and treasures to be sought
the more I see, the more I want
…I make for the hill in the distance.

51. *Broken clay.*

Wash this sin
make me as white as the heavens.
Cleanse this heart
unclog the clots of hate and wrath.
Weave in me a spirit pure,
filled with love and the hope to endure.
Mold me afresh, oh Potter above,
this clay is broken and has no worth.

52. The night's secret

If I openly kissed you
they would blatantly stare
close to yours
my lips should not appear
our forbidden union
they have made aware
a love like this
they would mercilessly tear
so I patiently wait
for the still silent night
to love and hold and caress you
fill your lips with delight.

53. Romeo.

Only you will understand
the words on this page
what we never had
will always be of age.

The truth is-
we were both afraid
engulfed so deep
our play, could not stage.

54. Unleashed

If they knew my thoughts
I would be banished.
…cast out into everlasting pain.

If they searched my heart
they would find love unexplained
so vast but sadly unclaimed.

If they saw my tears
their judgment they would refrain
a love like this, they can not tame.

55. My forbidden love

My forbidden love for you
slowly eats away
I know this love will not
birth a beautiful day
so I painfully pray,
as I painfully decay
that she will love you the same way.

I'm in love with you
silently I'm in love

I'm in love with you
hopelessly I'm in love.

Silently I hope that one day
you will love me endlessly
I'm in love.

57. I'll cry tomorrow.

Sorrow's darkness creeps into my heart's plains
breeding and burrowing thought these veins
this elegant spirit lies lifeless beneath these bones,
I'll cry tomorrow.

Not today, the pain is not enough for today
I'll wait for agony to build up behind these walls
so that it may plummet in torrents and in falls
my tears will crash as the thunder in the fall
I will cry tomorrow, for us all.

58.

Oh red setting sun
high in the clouds,
hearken your ear
as we cry from the ground.

Oh red setting sun
mighty and round,
why do you draw your hue
from my brothers around?

Oh red setting sun
you've sucked out our lives,
and now we lay dead
as you shed cranberries from the skies.

Oh red setting sun
you promised to rise- lead us,
now you only set behind the clouds
-you have deceived us.

59.

Love- heat.
Hearts- skip.
Skipping beats- rhythmically greet.
The buckle bleats to the skirt's slit
and as she reaches, he longingly kisses.
Tongues daintily dancing.
Silence.

60.

Your ship sets out into the dark pools of my eyes
- drawn into their cryptic passion.

Yearning echoes steal the air-
as your luscious lips refresh mine.

You set sail-
dragging your fingers along my neck's rivers
exploring every smooth winding surface
and plunge in torrents
into
     the
         bed
between the olive mountains.
Tall . . . inverted . . . tear drops . . .

Love invitingly directs your compass
and you briefly pause at the dip in my earth's belly
grazing its charming plain . . .
but the current calls and carries you on
and you are led to my india
and in there . . .